LILY!
HERE'S TO
TURNING TO
DARK OVER
OUR HANDS! HERE'S
TO WOLVES &
WILD DONG
L'CHAIM.

73

Slow Dance with Sasquatch
a collection of poetry

ભ

by Jeremy Radin

Write Bloody Publishing
America's Independent Press

Long Beach, CA

WRITEBLOODY.COM

Radin, Jeremy.
1ˢᵗ edition.
ISBN: 978-1-935904-53-3

Interior Layout by Lea C. Deschenes
Front Cover Designed and Painted by Blaine Fontana
Back Cover Designed by Bill Jonas
Author Photo by Derrick Brown
Proofread by Zhanna Vaynberg
Edited by Mindy Nettifee, Brian Ellis and Derrick Brown
Type set in Bergamo from www.theleagueofmoveabletype.com

Printed in Tennessee, USA

Write Bloody Publishing
Long Beach, CA
Support Independent Presses
writebloody.com

To contact the author, send an email to writebloody@gmail.com

MADE IN THE USA

For Kayla,
my sister,
my best hero,
my most friend

SLOW DANCE WITH SASQUATCH

SLOW DANCE WITH SASQUATCH

PART I
Love Letters to the Lord of Rooms

PART II
Sidewalk Chalk Monsters

PART I
LOVE LETTERS TO THE LORD OF ROOMS

*"May he be reincarnated as a chandelier
and hang by day and burn by night"*
—Yiddish curse

How It Is Made

In her absence he lays
with his blood-
less fist pulsing
against his chest.

His other hand,
in front of his mouth
so his breath curls
back and back and back.

In her absence
he invents her
and falls in love
with the inventing

as his friends
become husbands
and fathers.

BLIND RIFLER OF DOVES
after Shira Erlichman

This sadness, a sack of blind
doves, opened by a man
in a helicopter. I shoot at them, blind
too, blind rifler of doves, hands
full of rifles. The doves explode, light
the dusk with fireworks of flour. To-
morrow the yard is a stand of cake
trees. This sadness, an ascension

into bleached woods, a blind sack
of dead doves, rifle fingers
finding always the small hearts,
shivering bits of confetti, neighbor
children building houses in a forest
of my sorrow, climbing, biting
the necks of the cake trees, faces
bearded with frosting, my skin
a seed bag, overflowing
                    with bullets.

A Pyramid of Bison

Here is the home I have come back to
after my most magnificent failing.
My father's house at the end of the road.

Here is the brick staircase that leads to the front door.

Here is the part where I climb it again, pride
tucked like socks
into unworn work boots.

Here is the hallway that spits me into kitchen.
The clutter, the rainwater, sinking
through the ceiling. Crispex rooted. Dish crust
crusting. Rind. Stem. Knife.

Here is the refrigerator. White, woodless casket.
How many times have I buried myself in it?
Harmonizing with the humming 'til the lights burned
out. 'Til I dreamed of sex
amongst the pickles, the cream cheese.

Here is papa's credit card, lying on the table
so I do not go hungry or learn how to hunt.

Here is the couch that has memorized
the shape of me.

Here is the carpet that drinks deep the cream soda,
the barbecue sauce, the globs of cake frosting.

Here is the TV – furnace flicker mouth-king.
How many hours have I shoveled through
your yawn?

Here is the bedroom with nothing on the walls.
Pictures in frames on the closet floor. Collages
of songwriters, stuffed behind dressers.

Here is the bed. The one-man country. The quiet
war. Limp. Anthemless.

Here are my bloodlines, hardening in boxer briefs.

Here is a sock you could use as a boomerang.

Here is the mirror. The liar. The yes thief.

Here are bookshelves like buildings, stacked up with stories.
The books that I wish were a cold flock of shotguns.
How I long for the pages
to turn against my skull.

Here is the empty
and here is the empty.

Here are the secrets
and here are the secrets.

Here is the truth that I play hide and seek with.

Here are my sorrows – a pyramid of bison.
How did I ever stack heavy so high?

Here is where I murdered the men I wished to be:
Kite-eating loverboys, steel-skinned rain heroes,
bone-brushers, moon-pushers,
gruff pickers of pears.

What did we think we were trying to do?

Why did we ever think we could?

This house, it grins
like an autopsied carcass, says

*This is how I will always remember you: trembling
like an antelope brought down by arrows,
asking the arrows
if it's okay to bleed.*

So Speaks the Lord of Rooms

When the night pushes your head into its lap, chokes you with its yesless anatomy. When the whiskey is a bellyful of dark nails. When you never drink, but tonight is a fresh death, I am this night. When wicked tangle finds your hunger. When the high-heel party bullet-holes your brain, rakes across your nerves, this is me. When heavy hangs like blanket hell. When sleep mocks you from the corners of the room. When lust pushes its arm through the sleeve of your body. When your body becomes a room of mine that only I may enter, that only I may write the writing on the wall & know the writing. When the writing is *no, is no, is not you, not this time, you cannot say this.* I am this that you cannot say. Now say *hallelujah* & say *amen. Hallelujah* my spider-eyes falling from the ceiling. Your beds phantom-loaded, *hallelujah, amen.* Come to me. To the edge of yourselves. Fawns to a river. Cold sweet cold. I am this flowing steady bordering, this quench, this quench & quench, this wet thing pulling frigid through you. Bees in black jelly. Ribbon of unlit snow. When the orchards blaze. When the phone does not. When the phone is so quiet it sounds like your pulse. When you follow shame into the kitchen. When you guzzle the syrup. The honey anvils. The looping molasses, anchor chain heavy, I am this feeding, this filling, this crushing the bright beast. The rise-up. The ogre of light. When you are drunk on ghost fuel. Cooking the hope swans. Unbent. Unlusted. Unhoped. Unwild. The names of all of my names, sing them. Your voices blooming blister lovely, sing them. Your voices low, fastened to the mud, sing my names & I will be that singing, that mud, that rising, that hoping, that eating, that choking, that choking, that choking, that upside-down mountain lodged in your throat, pressing my names back into you.

WHILE IN THE SHOWER

Lace your fingers together
against your stomach.
Palms up. Make a bowl.
Let the water stream
over your shoulders,
down your torso,
into the bowl,
until your hands
are full of water.
Make sometimes
a shallow pool, sometimes
a deep, dark one –
the kind found in a cavern
nestled in the earth,
with blind white newts
and the air standing
still as herd of taxi-
dermied goats. Imagine
yourself tiny,
swimming in this pool
within your hands,
touching the bottom,
where the fingers
interlace, sitting and
sunning on the ridge
of your thumb.
Sometimes I will be
there too. Sometimes
the rain will touch you
with my fingers.
Feel the wrinkles
spreading over you.
Sweet, lonesome
pruning. Soon you will
be old again. Think
of all you've never

done. Let the water
fall to the floor,
burst like a chandelier.

OH, MOTHER!
after reading Leonard Cohen on the toilet

Oh, mother!

If I really knew
what I was doing

I'd be telling you
about all the women

instead of telling
all the women

about you.

All the Girls in Hollywood
Are Having the Same Dream

1.
In the woods, she can't run fast enough.
Stilettos caked in mud and sap, she falls to
the dirt, lays on her back,
rubs her feet against the bottom of space.
No matter how much mud she scrapes
on the stars, she can't get it all
off her shoes.

      He is gaining.

2.
In the city, she hides from dark
police officers, eating fireworks
behind a dumpster
beneath graffiti that says

     The gates are open.
     The wonder drug
        is wonder.

Colored lights blink in her belly.

3.
In Antarctica, planting a type of flower.
She farms them
for medicinal purposes. They turn her
blood to butterflies of violet
that float upwards from her wounds.

The wounds do not heal,
but she is too stunned
by their beauty
to notice.

4.
In a house of attics, she spends
the rest of her life
trying not to kiss the man who lives with her,
no matter how often he brews the tea
or brings her caramels.

Instead, she walks like a prison guard
through the secret rooms of secret rooms,
between small cages where she keeps the trees,
skinny and whimpering in her flashlight beam,
before flaying off their skins
for dance floors.

After Spending the Day Hitting the Gym and Jacking Off to Redtube

You get a text from that girl you met at Saddle Ranch.
She just got off work and you should
bring a bottle of something strong
over to her apartment.
You roll on deodorant, step into your True Religions,
haul ass over to CVS
and an hour later, you're sitting on her couch,
whiskey fireflying behind your eyeballs,
tongue cat-burglaring more liquor
from her jewelry box mouth.
You curl a fist around a breast
until the hummingbirds start
scrambling. You rip her
panties, think of the dress
your mother used to parade you
around in when she held
your boy letters in her mouth
like a bar of soap. Feel it falling
from you now. Undo the buttons that have fastened you
to gentleness. You can show this girl, this canvas
for your ghost paint. Teach her the secret
language of men. Tell her
with your whole strength
what we talk about in bathrooms,
alone. Pound her into steaming,
yowling, naked, red submission. Lay
your train tracks straight through her pretty
pink mansion. Look at your reflection.
You're doing so good. Your cock
is a chainsaw, an industry of axe blades. Take her
jungle apart. All her slender trees,
reams of paper
you will cover with your name.

THIS HEAVEN OF MUD

Lord, bless this inelegant sadness.
Bless the sorrow that has smuggled me
into its dingy cabin.

Bless the plates of food it leaves out for me.
Bless the quiet baths it draws for me.
Bless the beds and the space inside them.

Lord, bless the empty rooms.
All these empty rooms.

Bless the panic that shakes me like a bone in its jaws.
Bless the fear, the crush of gut anvils.
The worry, snow-packed in my wishing well throat.

Bless the temper, Lord. Grinding
traffic, fist through windshield, head
through sunroof, boot through dashboard,
my mother's chest.

Bless the smoke-spine girls I hunt for you
in the eyes of.
Bless the lust for their salt, their lemons.
Bless their fingernails lodged
in the walls of my aorta.
Bless the ones who climbed safely
away from my obsession.

Bless the mistakes, your finest achievement.
Holy: the lost wallet. Forgotten stovetop.
Longing's insistence
that I'm ready to love. All your creaking
lock bust music, opening my blood.

Bless my greasy blood, Lord, dump-trucked through my veins.
My clay-thick, garbage-sick blood, Lord, bless it.
Bless my muscles, soft as prom queen thigh satin.
Bless my skeleton, swaddled in fat. This heavy ruin,

bloated sarcophagus, bacon-wrapped
funeral body, Lord, bless it half to death
and bless it again.

Bless the black daffodils my skin is sewn around.
Heaving toward sunlight, bloating my flesh.
All this shriveled beauty, Lord.
Bless the kitchen knives that salmon
upwards from my lungs, slicing up these prayers
before they reach the back of my tongue.

Lord, bless my tongue and the songs buried in it,
this holy howling bedroom gospel.
Chewing grief into a mouthful of accordions.
Bless the accordions, Lord, bury me in accordions.
That my last gasp may be one note
in a harmony of hinges, a chord plucked
by the great, swelling beast of heaven,
a note in a song that will sound like a life,
that will fill the mouth with chocolate,
Lord, bless the chocolate.
Bless the chocolate.

Bless this necessary sadness,
this miraculous sadness,
this gigantic absence,
this heaven of mud,
stampeding like music
down into the empty spots.
Bless the empty spots.
Bless the empty.

The uncoveted, unbent,
unlusted, unhoped, unwild.
Bless the depression farmers,
suicide gardeners,
lonesome priests
of the church
of the Lord of Rooms, Lord,
bless me.

Bless me with your tusks,
your claws,
your fangs,
your jaws,
tear me apart, Lord,
bless me with the tearing –
I am ready for the tearing,
I am ready for the tearing,
the tearing,
the tearing,
bless me with the tearing,
Lord, scatter me through the field
until I sink into the dirt.

Until trees begin to grow from me.

Until rivers begin to begin from me.

Until I am nothing
but a disaster of seeds
glowing in the bellies of crows.

PART II
SIDEWALK CHALK MONSTERS

"Children in the sand outside
on their hands and knees,
sketching pictures all day long
of stranger things than these"
—John Darnielle, "Tianchi Lake"

THE INN OF THE PURPLE BISON

Hello, traveler.
Welcome to The Inn of the Purple Bison.
The bread is just now rising in the oven.
The tapers are lit; they smell of nutmeg
and orange peel. The stew on the stove
has been cooking all day long. There is
a man on the porch who plays a piano.
We don't know where he came from.
He brought the piano. We've all brought
such heavy things to this place. We have
all come here to rest from the carry. The
chairs in the lobby are built from yarn.
Hot chocolate moves through canals in
the floor. The mattresses, stuffed with the
softest fog. A bloodhound sleeps by every
fireplace. Their dreams, projected on the
bedroom walls. The blessing fields. The
sky full of rabbits. Look how the road has
etched your face, spit its body into your
hair. We have found a blue petal that
works like water. Come and lie in the
cleansing lather. What you have done out
there is not our concern. All that you have
tangled and cut. All that you have turned
against. All the wars you have made and
loved. All the wounds you have nursed
and fed. All that you have too easily killed.
All that you could not help but kill. Start
fresh. Start here. Welcome to The Inn of
the Purple Bison. We know what the night
has done to you.

SEED

The boy sits next to his imagination. No!
The imagination sits next to his boy. No!
The boy sits *inside* his imagination. No!
The *imagination* sits *inside his boy. No!*

All of the swans are swallowing shotguns. Yes!
The leaves of all trees are leprechauns, hiding. Yes!
When the cupboard is closed, the teacups are dancing. Yes!
The bookcase is made from the spine of an ogre. Yes!
The ogre is made from the chair and the shadow, yes!
The shadow is made from the moon and the sweater, yes!
The window is made from the skin of the desert!

Yes!   *Yes!*   *Yes!*

The desert is made from the sneeze of the hippo!
The hippo is made from the size of a story!
The story is made from the hair of a moment!
The moment is made from the ghost of a heartbeat!

Heartbeat built from the breath of a biscuit,
biscuit bloomed from the music box belly,
music box born from the pit of a dragon,
pit of the dragon a cardboard suitcase,

a suitcase that carries a love poem to axe blades,
an axe blade that carries a love poem to young blood,
a young blood that carries a love poem to daylight,
a daylight that carries a love poem to love poems,

a love poem that carries the shape of a trigger,
the trigger you press and it lives you forever –

forever is made from a song that keeps skipping,
forever is made from a skip that keeps rising,
forever is made from a rise that keeps highing,

a bread that keeps feeding a bolt that keeps leading
a boat that keeps flipping a bell that keeps tripping
a dust that keeps whipping a horse that keeps ripping
a seed that keeps seeding a seed that keeps seeding

a room in the city where someone is sitting

where someone is sitting and not saying nothing.

PERHAPS A THOUSAND YEARS

Upon waking,
I was a curved sword
in the grasp
of an Arabian prince.

Tonight, I am all of the cheeseburgers
in Canoga Park.

Throughout the day
I was also these things:

a goose with spoons for feathers.

A pair of old moccasins
with blood on the toe.

A braid in the hair of a young woman
descended from gypsies
texting in line at a Starbucks.

There have also been days,
long before this one,
perhaps a thousand years,
where I have been

a crossbow that shoots Whoopie Cushions,
Magic cards,
bubbles,

a barrel of jacks
in the belly of a tiger shark,

a beer bottle sweating
between the thighs
of a sorority girl,

a basket
of purple powder,

the workstation of a man
who does monster make-up
for the movies.

Tonight, however, I am still
all of the cheeseburgers
in Canoga Park

and tomorrow morning
I am hoping
I wake up.

BIRDHOUSES

Birdhouses were used to replace her lungs the winter she got sick. Her grandson found her in bed, coughing ketchup onto her pink, padded nightgown. Mommy and daddy were at work so it was up to him. It was a good thing he'd gotten the doctor bag for Hanukkah.

"Deep breath, Gramma!" He listened with the bright blue and yellow stethoscope. "Gramma, did you recently swallow any rattlesnakes?"

"No my dear, but 'recently' is a very good word."

"Why does it sound like that when you breathe?"

"Well my dear, Grandma has very old lungs."

"Want me to make you new ones?"

"That would be lovely."

He worked all day. Glued popsicle sticks into a pair of cabins, colored them with markers. One was swirls of orange, purple, pink, peach, and blue, roof thatched with pine needles, dinosaurs glued down, standing guard at the door. The other was green.

"How do we put them in, Gramma?"

"Well, you're going to have to cut me open, like the hunter in the wolf story. The only thing sharp enough are these magic scissors. They're invisible. Now who wants to see what the inside of a grandma looks like?"

"But I never cut somebody open before, what if I hurt you!"

"Well then, why don't I do it?"

And she snip-snip-snipped under the blanket until it was time to put the birdhouses in. After she sewed herself back up, he uncovered his eyes.

"Good as new, my darling. Thank you."

She kissed her fingers, touched them to his forehead, held them there for a long, long time. They were cool and soft as new birthday candles. The smell of potatoes and medicine.

The next morning, he awoke to a banging in her room. He found her still as cotton candy, bird after bird crashing like dizzy angels into the window.

CHICKEN STORM

Musta been like a thousand chickens come flyin' up from the other side'a that hill. I spent my whole life knowin' them chickens couldn't fly & then here they come, a sunrise'a crazy brown feathers, up from the other side'a that hill. Ain't no explanation for it, I know that. My wife, well, she stood next t'me, squeezed my hand & said oh kinda soft, as the chickens p'kew-wwwwed into the clouds. They disappeared in them clouds. Then the next thing, there's eggs everywhere, fallin' from the sky. & each time them eggs hit the ground & burst like watermelons, there'd be more chickens. Tiny chickens – but not chicks, y'see, grown-up adult chickens, but tiny like yer fist or yer knee or a cup'a coffee, that'd go zoomin' up after them original chickens & droppin' eggs'a their own & then tinier chickens came from them eggs & so on & so forth til there's chickens the size'a houseflies & dust mites & most likely chickens ya can't even see & we're standin' baffled in a hurricane'a chickens or dust cloud'a chickens or like a flashflood'a chickens. & in the barn the horses are screamin' like they got necks full'a devils. Just stampin' their hooves & screamin', like maybe scared out their damn minds. Or maybe like us. Me & this woman, my wife, whose ticker's a good onion, who's pressin' her lips t'my lips in the middle'a this chicken storm like maybe we always been this young.

THE LAST INVITATION
Sept. 5th, 1895

My Dear Theodore,

October approaches. I can smell it now, from my place beneath
the wind chimes; a rough scent; a hunkering down; a preparation.

It would be my honor to receive you for the coming hunt.
There has been, in my life, nothing to match the power of it.
The bears don't die like other animals. When the knife bites
into their pulse, you can see them understand.

At first, I did not weep when their blood rushed
down my arm. The blood of bears
is not like the blood of other animals; it is a spirit
blood, angry with the scent of hickory.

My pigs were happy.

It started as a vengeance game, you see; the bears, they came
and slaughtered my happy pigs. Charcoal demons, hurtling
through the canebrakes. I took the hounds to find them.
When we did, we descended

upon them, righteous, upon the mothers, the cubs, the husbands.
I cut them down in wide, ragged strokes, my broad blade clutched
like a tornado in the Lord's hand. The blood, so heavy.

We ate them, Theodore. Joked loudly as we turned
them into bacon. Have you ever eaten bear? The flesh
is not like other animals. Days later you can still feel it

gushing through your system. Hunting the parts of you
that feel proud and tall and male.

These are sacred animals. Their eyes, you should see the way
they look into you, what do they know that they lie so still,
so tranquil and easy as you open their necks like doors?
Theodore, we are on the inside of something, we are trapped,
we are blind in here

and the bears
are the way out.

The men had to pull me from the last one; I'd climbed into his neck
almost to my shoulders. The things I saw while my head was submerged
in all that meat, Mr. President...

may I call you Mr. President? May I speak of the future
of this country, written across my eyes in bear's blood?

Mr. President,
I saw an old farmer tending to a harvest of bullets.
I saw a river of barbed wire moving through the bodies of infants.
I saw trees skinned alive, tattooed with the faces of prostitutes,
your hands, Mr. President, I saw them stitching the wounds
of this country with its own entrails. I saw you heal its mind
(when it was the soul was failing), I saw you shouting
in the streets of Wisconsin, Delaware, Iowa

but nobody was listening, I saw you roaring like a wounded moose;
your pain, loud as cannons, but nobody was listening. I saw you swinging
bison around your head, hurling them through the doors of the church
but nobody was listening. You stomped and spit and cursed

but nobody was listening. The hounds came for you, and men
shaped like hunting blades cut you from their memories, you rode
a bear into the forest and both your throats were bleeding
and you wept, Mr. President.

Oh, how you wept
as you played that piano. The one they carved into your teeth.
The teeth they carved into the side of that mountain.

You touched the keys as if you meant to
bury some dream behind them, inside the great, wide grave
of your mouth.

All of these things you will witness, when you are baptized
in the carcass of the animal, taking its wet hell into your lungs.

My Dear Theodore,

It would be an honor to receive you for the coming hunt,
if you can find us, down amongst the canebrakes, in the cellar
of this country.

We are lost in this country.

Wearing the blood of beasts
as a wedding dress.

Fattening our bellies
with the bodies of gods.

GIRL DANCES LIKE A SUFI IN A LIT FIELD AS SOMEONE OFF-CAMERA BLOWS BUBBLES

after a photograph by Michelle Nunes

Hemmed in by globes of soap, lifting
swan arms into sky.
Each globe, a thin-skinned ball-

room, chandeliered, dizzy with
emeralds. Spring erupting into bits
of buzzing jewelry. So much sooner than

she knows, the snow will return; count-
less astronauts becoming lakes, ghosts,
astronauts. The bubbles knit them-

selves around her. She is
rabbi, blooming sufi, shining
hound dog. The moon rolling in her

mouth, burning away the black-
ness. Cocoa eyes half-closed. Lips
parted. A song builds its body

within her, a psalm
not even the snow can say.

A Book of Poems for Miriam Stone

Mother,

Such a strange thing has been happening. It began in the summer. I had gone outside to retrieve the mail and noticed that there was only a piece of paper in the mailbox, brittle and delicate. No bills, coupons or magazines, only this old piece of paper. Written upon it was a poem:

The August sun is a bundle of ivory
hawks. Today, they have flown down to land
on your shoulders. Your old, yellow
housecoat, it cannot hide
the things I know. The sky,
merely something for your skin
to be brighter than. This wide mouth
of sun, wishing to hold you
         like a cub in its teeth.

I stopped reading and looked around. There was no one there. I did not know what to do. Mother, it was the first day of August and I was wearing an old yellow housecoat. Was someone playing a trick on me? Had the mailman become enamored with me? He seems to be a lonely man, perhaps even older than I. Trembling, I read on, and then my pulse was so violently fast I thought my breast would splinter. The next part went like this:

It is not too late for you. To die
alone is not your business here.
You are a creature of warm dust, of bloom
in dark places. Pull the pins
of jade from your hair, let it unfurl, a pale
carpet rushing down the courtyard of
your back. An avalanche
of snow angels. I will speak
these words within you, untether
the horses. The flowers, trampled, rainbow
powder falling from your wrists.

I took the paper inside, clutched very tightly to my chest. I didn't know if I wanted it to be real. I put it on the bedside table. That night, I did not think I would sleep. But oh, mother, how I slept! Better than I have slept in thirty years. I dreamt of a man with the face of a hawk and I was beautiful beneath his palms. He was making love to me in a room that was burning. When I woke I was naked, hair down, slick with sweat. The house was quieter than it has ever been. I went to the mailbox and again, there was only an old piece of paper, like the first:

And yes, and how you wore those moths
in your limbs, and yes, and how I felt
wings beneath my tongue,
wings beneath the goose-flesh,
this flight that you have taken will not be
            the last, yes, I will
come for you raw, bending round
your bones, pouring
myself into you, wrapping your voice
in tender thunder. Immaculate smoke.
We are matches in a museum of clocks.

And it has gone on like this for nearly fifty days. Nothing in the mail but poem after poem. This is no trick. This has nothing to do with the mailman. Something very strange is happening, mother. There is a book on the nightstand. It has been written for me. As if the years had decided to make up for all this lost time, mother, these are poems that tell my life; secrets I've never told. They move through me, filling me with dreams. And what is happening to my body... it has been so long, so much longer than I can say. I had forgotten what these muscles were made for, what a sweetness I could become. What a perfect sweetness.

Today, this came:

At midnight, come again
        to the mailbox...

It is midnight now, mother. The mailbox is open.
Somehow, it is large enough to step inside of.
Candles are burning along the walls.
There is a door.

I love you very much.

Miriam

OFF-SWITCH

There was once a boy
who stayed up far past his bedtime,
trembling.

He could hear murderers
coming up the stairs
with kid-guts
hanging from their knives.

The tree outside his window
bubbled with devils,
the stars were fire-spiders
unwinding their legs toward Earth,
the neighbor's dogs
were shape-shifting boy thieves,
waiting for him
to fall asleep.

So he rolled out of bed,
spilled his Legos on the floor,
built an off-switch
for all the things that hunted him.

And just for good measure,
with what was left over,
he built four force-field generators,
placed them at the corners of his bed,
got under the covers
with the rifle
he'd gotten from Disneyland,
told the night
just what would happen
if it tried to come for him again.

He slept in such peace –
a beach of soft, white sand
washed gently by waves

of polar bears, river otters,
banjo strings, purple lava.

The next morning,
he told his mommy and daddy
how he had out-smarted
and out-fearsomed
the murderers,
fire-spiders,
tree-devils,
and boy-thieves.

They became worried.

So they called a doctor,
told him all
that their son had told them,
and the doctor said

No, no, no!
The mind of a child
is no place for a child!

And gave them an orange bottle
full of off-switches
that looked like little yellow Pacmen

that ate all the ghosts
in his imagination
and when they were done
eating the ghosts

they ate the rest of his imagination too.

PART III
BANJO CAKE AT THE SEDER TABLE

"Seedlings turn overnight to sunflowers,
blossoming even as we gaze"
—Sheldon Harnick, "Sunrise, Sunset", *Fiddler on the Roof*

CAREER PATH OF A NINE-YEAR-OLD
after Mindy Nettifee

I wanna be a wolf.
I have a book with them hunting moose in Alaska.
I hunt lizards on the soccer field while everyone
else plays basketball.
I can outrun any lizard or even deer or even
anybody in my whole grade
except Donald C. so I wanna be a baseball player
like Ricky Henderson.
He steals all the bases. I wanna steal the voice
of Kevin. I wanna steal the words he calls me.
One day they'll run from my bicep muscles
& get scared of my face paint.
One day I'll bodyslam 'em right when they
shoot out of his mouth
so I wanna be a wrestler. I practice sleeper holds
on the pillows when it's past my bedtime.
I can't sleep 'cause there's a force-field around my bed
that keeps the sleep out. Which I even told the doctor
with the green sweater
who makes me draw pictures & only has nine hairs
that make his head look like a super shiny zebra
& he said he could help
but I don't know what little orange pills
can do about a FORCE-FIELD
so I wanna be a *force-field specialist.*
Maybe when I'm a grown-up they'll have real live
force-fields. I wish they had 'em now.
I wish I had one when my friends dared my little sister
to punch me in the face on the baseball diamond.
I bled like someone in a shark movie.
I bled like I had a bull shark also known as
a Zambeze shark trapped in my face,
eating its way out of my face & then everybody laughed
& I couldn't turn invisible no matter how hard I closed
my eyes, so I wanna be a wizard.

Then I'd have invisibility powers
& other powers like flying & wisdom
& a pet dragon who wouldn't let anyone laugh at me.
His name would be "Raptor Laser Death Volcano Radin".
I love dragons. I can draw the ones that live
in the hills next to the freeway. We moved
away from my old house & I brought them with me
& now they guard my room.
They have arrows for eyelashes that can shoot
& grow back &
scorpion tails made of diamond material
but black diamond material 'cause
black is *scary* & the tail can shoot poison or acid
& they have teeth made out of laser beams &
instead of just normal fire they breathe
bats that are on fire
that they can control with telepathy.
The only thing scarier
is Ritalin. He's a little yellow knight.
He cuts their heads off & buries them in the dirt
so I wanna be a paleontologist. I always lose things.
Maybe I could dig 'em up.
If I dig deep enough, maybe I could find things
other people lost too
like how mommy & daddy used to love each other
& I could even put it back together but I wouldn't
put it in a museum.
Maybe it got buried when the big earthquake came.
The one that broke my gramma's house
& my friends' houses & the houses of everyone else
standing on the streets of Chatsworth
like dropped ice cream cones.
I wish I could gather all of them up & keep them safe.
I have so much room so… I wanna be a house.
But I'm bigger than a house.
So maybe I could be a library.
& everyone could come in & read about things so amazing
they'll forget about all the things they lost
& then maybe when they're done & looking

for something new to read,
they'll stumble upon that book about wolves.
The one that says how they talk to each other
better than we do.
How they're not talking to the moon, like I thought,
but to each other,
teaching the other wolves everything they know
about what goes on in these old, dark woods.
So I wanna be a wolf.
I wanna be a wolf
so when my little sister asks me
why everything is changing,
& what's out there,
& why does God
keep running away
& coming back
& running away
& coming back
& why do our hearts do this
even when
we don't ask them to,
I'll know exactly what to say.

Arms and Horses

Once, as I wept in his arms, my father sang
to me. The song, a necklace of coins
unspooling from his beard, piling up on the carpet.
His beard, black as wet hooves.
He dreams of horses, his favorite
movie: *The Black Stallion*.
Once, his mother warned him of the world's
secret horrors: Stampedes! Reefer! The snarling
house beneath swaying skirts! My grandmother,
tough as Clydesdale meat,
pulls me onto the dance floor.
Someone has been *bat mitzvahed*
and I am so small, a pitcher of grape juice,
tilting, tilting, staining her paper
arms. My father watches us dance, beams
of light growing
from his shoulders, projecting
films onto the reception hall ceiling:
a horse the color of a horse's
pupil drowns
in a river of dry cleaning.
Once, I found him weeping on the floor of
the kitchen, bulldozed by stress, a plate
in three pieces. I lift his tiny body
into my thirteen-year-old arms, begin to sing
a song of lemon trees,
polish for the saddle, a temple
that slowly fills with water.

Thirteen Things That Happen When My Father Snores

1.
The cat hides.

2.
My sister closes his door, mutters
as she walks back down the hall,
lays in bed,
flickers like a candle.

3.
Every window dances. The stars they hold
vibrate, drunk.

4.
A Kodiak bear wrestles a silverback gorilla.
And three warthogs.
In a volcano.
On a comet.

5.
Geysers on Jupiter erupt with hot chocolate,
the hot chocolate freezes in the icy yawn of space,
galaxies of new chocolate planets are born.

6.
Autumn runs through thin black trees,
its arms outstretched.

7.
A man inside a man's head
plays golf on the sun.

8.
Welcome...*to Jurassic Park!*

9.
Our house opens its palms,
holds the night like a dying blackbird.

10.
Children sit in lawn-chairs, wrapped in blankets,
drinking Coke through straws,
watching sparks twirl in the second story window.

11.
A green feather rises
into the sky
forever.

12.
Burglars choose a different house.

13.
A man sleeps.
He dreams of whales spinning
through an ocean of sawdust.
His children are safe.

Don't the Moon Look Lonesome

Morry sings a song as he builds the grandfather clock.
Don't the moooooooooon look lonesome...

Alone in the garage, flanked by aging tools
and daddy long-legs, he caresses the wood
like it's a woman
who offers up her edges to be smoothed
while his wife chews the lust from her knuckles
in the kitchen.

Neither remembers the last time
they'd been touched.

Finally finished, the grandfather clock stands
in the living room, heralding the hours of
a dying marriage. Bessie stares at
it, imagines it as the building where old men
in old sweaters with strange old accents
build time.

The big dish hangs in the clock's abdomen.
Don't the moooooooooon look lonesome...

Silent at the dinner table, Morry dreams
of building airplanes in a forest of bonsai trees,
teaching his children the gifts of
hunger, taking a woman with feathers
as black
as Korean hair.

A woodsaw once took away most of his
wedding ring finger. Sometimes he puts the other
half up his nose. The children laugh and laugh.
Bessie does not laugh.
She dreams of being bent over the sink
as she does the dishes.

As he lies dying in his bed, she puts her ear
to his chest. She hears the sound of bombers
dropping ordnance on a city of laundry machines.
Slowly, he takes her hand. His voice
is dusty in his neck.

When I pass, don't let them put those coins on my eyes.
They look too much like moons.
I don't want to be alone anymore.

The night he dies, Bessie shoves the grandfather clock
as hard as she can. It seems to fall
in slow motion. Three matches later, it lights up
like an idea.

Soon the fire spreads to the carpet, the drapes,
the furniture he had built. When it begins
to move up the walls, she walks
outside. She stands in the front yard,
watches the house burn.

The clock, the workshop, the kitchen, her husband,
turning to ash,
dancing into the hills.

The Winter King
for Grandpa Bernie

I.
Devouring bowl after bowl of spaghetti in the big chair,
you holler at the Dodgers again. *Come on, Hershiser! What
the hells'a'matter with you?! Throw a goddamn strike!*
Grandma's Bolognese, quivering in your beard. I crawl
into the room. *HI, JEREMY!* You roar my name with your
entire body, whisk me up onto your lap. I dig my small digits
into the cloud on your face, that walloping thunder factory.
I decide that someday, I will have one of my own. You kiss
my cheek and your breath smells of Parmesan, dried oregano,
photographs with yellow edges, your fingers still ripe with
grandma's hairspray, and though I am young and do not
understand why, this makes me glad. Grandma's hair is
the color of a sleeping fox. Yours, a pack of polar bears.
Things that survive, the snow be damned.

III.
After you pass, I learn that an easy way to make grandma cry
is to do a play where I paint my beard white and wear big,
square glasses. I am you. Look at my hands. I am you.

II.
At the nursing home, grandma dissolves. A pile of faded rain-
bows and sea water. You mistake the staff for the ghosts of
bitter brothers, your children for old sweethearts, grandchildren
for empty bank accounts. I'm not sure if I'm allowed to feel
anything. How do you feel anything that's not about girls who
just want to be friends? I stand near my mother, her face a
full shopping bag with a wet bottom, ready to release, release.
You open your bombed graveyard of a mouth and weep,
silent, against the confusion. This is how I learn about grief:
the king of winter shrinking in a threadbare cardigan. This
is how I learn about God: a hunter balanced on the skid of
a helicopter, shooting at the legs of bears.

MAMA'S SECRET INGREDIENT LIST FOR HALLELUJAH SOUP

8 cups of chicken stock
3 bunches of parsley, torn by hand
3 onions, chopped
2 carrots, chopped
2 stalks of celery with leaves intact, chopped
6 cloves of garlic, crushed
Salt & pepper to taste
11 years of cut out t-shirt tags
6 strips of turquoise Doc Marten leather
3 lines of ram's horn powder
2 drawers of frilly holiday socks
1 box of secret peanut butter cereal
Confettied pages of a dinosaur novel
Shards of a mirror smeared with stage makeup
The jingle jangle of silver bracelets
The sand of evening's awful empire
Fistfuls and fistfuls of semi-colons
The rock I launched through the kitchen window
The curses sharpened on the whetstones in her ears
Her swollen heart
Our names
An unanswered telephone

DONUT MUFFIN

On the Food Network, they're talking about
the Donut Muffin from the Downtown Bakery and Creamery
in Healdsburg, California. A woman
bakes donut batter in a muffin tin, paints on
clarified butter, rolls them in maple and cinnamon. The roof
of my mouth is caving in.

Do not speak to me of aftermath.

Aftermath is lunchtime.

The day I learned of my diabetes, I drove
thirty minutes to Earl's Donuts
for two buttermilk bars and a maple bar. And a bear claw.
I have written suicide notes with frosting
stolen from the wedding cake
my body will never allow me to digest.

I am what will kill me.
Every single time.

According to Mapquest, I'm only seven
hours away from a partner in all of this.
From a sweet, golden-brown lover
who will bless my hurt,
marvel with me at the astonishing
power of my helplessness.

Do not speak to me of aftermath.

Aftermath is naptime.

Let me sleep, finally,
in the arms
of something beautiful.
Let me say my last
Fuck yous
with honey in my mouth.

MY HEART ATTACK ARRIVES

Lie your ass back down. Where you think
you're gonna go? Running was never your
strong suit. Really, how 'bout we don't pretend
you ain't been asking me to come here, praying
for something dark and mean to find you.
The firework show at the end of the pity party.
I have sent my ghosts before me to pass
like zephyrs through your pulse. I know you felt it.
The days it fluttered so bad, you thought about
the right way to apologize to everyone.

I am a hundred tons of C-4, strapped to your
plasma. The death of the emerging beat. The self-
destruct sequence ticking as the predator dies
inside you. I crushed the center of your grandfathers,
laid them out before their sixtieth birthdays.
They ran; I caught them. Better men than you.

Who are you? A day job. A cold call. I am the process
server, the one who never loosens the tie. I take.
I will find you. Silly fat boy. Sad revolutionary.
I've seen so many just as you are. You wanted
to teach them to love something ugly. To make them
laugh with all of their wild. To be full, so full,
like it meant something passionate and Russian.
To change their hearts, you have neglected
your own. You wanted to be everywhere.
To get so big, you disappear.

Wasps' Nest

We are shouting at each other in the kitchen.
She's just baked a tray of cookies.

I can't let you do this is what I'm saying.
What she's saying is that there's nothing I can do
to stop her. If I throw them away,
she'll only make more.

When she was fifteen, she told us
she wanted to stop eating
until she became
a ribbon of vapor, skinny
as a page in a fashion magazine.

YOU DON'T UNDERSTAND! THE WASPS WITHIN ME!
THE UNBROKEN STINGING! THE TERRIBLE STINGING!
THEY STING AND THEY STING AND THEY
DO NOT DIE!

She once tried to release them from her legs
with a nail clipper. Now she traps them
in the food, pulls the trigger
in her gullet, fires them
into the garbage disposal. She prays
there's no blood, drinks large bottles of water
to wash away the stingers.

Tonight, a tray of cookies on the counter.
Her face has gone
porcupine, bristling with razorblades.

JEREMY! I'M PUTTING MYSELF INTO A FUCKING
INPATIENT PROGRAM TOMORROW!
JUST LET ME DO THIS!

Fine! Just know that I won't be able to sleep tonight, knowing you're doing
what you're doing!

She says she doesn't give a fuck.

I say she's a selfish bitch.

Then I go upstairs
and the whole house starts to buzz.

WHEN MY TEN-YEAR-OLD COUSIN ASKS WHY I'M SO FAT

Because I weigh a lot. Because I forgot to go to the gym…for twenty-eight years in a row. Because the Jews have too many holidays. Because boogers are really hard to digest. Because ten-year-old boys are really hard to digest. Because I am saving up for the single greatest fart of all time. Because anxiety attacks don't count as exercise. Because now I can touch boobies whenever I want. Because free ham is *not* a Jewish dilemma, it's ham and it's free. Because nothing feels as good as skinny tastes. Because fast food is cheap and everywhere, just like me. Because Earl's Donuts, Brent's Deli, Umami Burger, More Than Waffles, Mulberry St. Pizza, the other Brent's Deli, The Counter, CiCi's, Chi-Chi's, Vin Loi, Big Mo's, Rib Ranch, Cavaretta's, THAT'S JUST THE SAN FERNANDO VALLEY.

Because what in this world tells you to *not* be hungry? Because never be fat but always be hungry! Because I was a little boy once and it wasn't enough. Because it is never enough. Because it was either eat or listen. Because how else to knit the crumble back together? Because how else to push the explosion back down? Because how else to muffle the rising surrender? Because what's the difference between *celebrate* and *grieve*? Because the lifeguard said *If you want to keep swimming, you're going to have to put your bikini top back on, young lady.* Because a gentle girl kissed my stretch marks and I dumped her the next morning. Because no matter how loud I bullied that boy, I couldn't unhear the ghouls in the mirrors. Because so much of my *so much* I have not yet learned to give.

Because I am a suitcase of mud-pies and bullet-holes, some days, a suitcase of swan feathers and sunrises. Because I am pregnant with yes, with champion dance moves, river monsters, the dreams of helicopters, my father's bones. Because there are such orchards unfolding within me – take this fruit, this fruit, sweet nourish, it is yours, let it fill you. Because I must carry this feeling always so that I don't start buying into what I see in magazines, billboards, the eyes of the club girls. Because most days there is nowhere for all this music to go. Because right after God said *LET THERE BE LIGHT*, He said *OH CRAP. I MADE TOO MUCH. WHAT AM I GOING TO DO WITH ALL THIS*

EXTRA LIGHT? Then He was like *I KNOW! LET THERE BE FAT PEOPLE!* Because this is how fat I have to be in order to hold how much I love you. Because I haven't used up all my *I love yous* yet and this is where I keep them. Because I know you didn't mean it. Because you're ten. Because you haven't stopped following me around since I got here. Because it's dinnertime and the soup is on the stove and the bread is on the table and the brisket's in the oven and I am already stuffed with the blueprints of stars that I am going to build for you.

PIPE ORGAN OWL MANSION
for Sister

"...a girl, already loved, already loud in the house of herself"
-Anne Sexton

"Well, that's the end'a this suit"
-Man being dragged through mud by a horse, Blazing Saddles

This is the year you begin.
The year you unbutton the pinstripe disease.
This is the year you turn around in the woods,
walk away from the grinding coyotes.
This is the year of the car crash stilettos.
This is the year of the *hallelujah* ballgown.
The diamond spill. The party dress.

This is the year you begin.
Unlearn the dead language of mirrors.
Whale hips. Walrus thighs.
These plump fictions, gasping like fish in a freezer.
This is the year you swallow the airplanes,
the spring geese, the mayfly soiree.
Fly hard toward the new water.
Bathing-suited.
Draped in sun blush and boy whistles.

This is the year you begin.
Slip into the sweet mud.
Get dirty.
Stay dirty.
There is nothing to forgive.

This is the year you begin.
You will lose no more fingers to the gullet demons.
Surrender no longer to your smart Jewish moods,
your insistent bathwater quiet.
You will rage with birdsong.
Be a nation of hysterical kookaburras.

Be a pipe organ owl mansion.

This is the year you begin.
You will bust through this bright Funfetti sadness.
You will upside-down avalanche.
Shake in the footlights like an unhinged priestess.
Walk with mistletoe strung from your eyelashes.
Look into every mirror you can find.
Dance with our mother in the gowns of free women.
Open the sensational hell in your belly.
Let us in.
The world is ready to fall in love with you.

This is the year you begin.
You will romance with elegance and steady grace.
You will feast and adore yourself for feasting.
You deserve the feast.
You deserve the feast.

This is the year you begin.
More beautiful than the honey-tendril debutantes,
the whip willow dancers,
the lingerie beasts, the switchblade sisters.
More beautiful than the shiny thing
that hangs on the front of the Torah
and all the shame
that squats and snarls behind it.
More beautiful than the art
of accurate suffering.
More beautiful than fear.
More beautiful than mama's absence,
papa's solitude, my impatience, the body
you yearn for. The perfect smoke, the shape of the smoke,
more beautiful than death.
You are more beautiful than death.

PART IV
SLOW DANCE WITH SASQUATCH

*"So you see, dogs like us, we ain't
such dogs as we think we are"*
—Paddy Chayevsky, *Marty*

Aviary Mouth

Next door lives the girl with the aviary
mouth. The white barns in my gums,
I want them loaded with owls.

I don't sleep anymore. Haunted by her
birds. They move the night
with their wings. They warble and die.

The gravity crushes me into the sheets.
I will hang myself from the telephone
wires. She will come for me then.

She will pluck out the dark. She will
carry me up through the crumbling sky.

GERMAN SNOW

Somewhere in Germany, bundled up against
the hollow winter, you will think
of me. The frost, a wedding dress

you no longer wish to wear.
Lay with me in California, together
in the mango sun. I will take my shirt off.

I trust you. The frost doesn't. Come
pray to the cartwheeling birds:
Birds, make me beautiful. Make my flesh

bloom; rugged. Shirtless. Animal
lightning. Make me tiny, so tiny, that I may sleep
forever on the black hammocks of

her eyelashes. Make me snow. Fill the ocean
with my body. Let me walk across myself to her.
Tonight, the distance is incredible.

So easy to give up on. You
are so far away, I can almost hear you
behind me. The miles

between us stand up, a fat man
made of mountains, plains, seawater.
His vocal chords, pillars of German snow.

Koi

Finally, alone at the bar. Me, her haircut, her high-
heels, the pastel sparrows inked

above her breasts. She says something funny,
I say *shut up*, she says *you shut up*, we look at each other

for a long,   l o n g time. I watch as
her mouth hangs open; an unanswered

question. Later, she shows me the koi fish on
her thigh, revealing her panties, the pale peak of hip

I will spend two years imagining the taste of. Surely
something soaked in bayou wine. Her name, the swamp

wind going down on the willows. I will search
for her on Facebook

the nights I forget to be proud of my loneliness.
Driving home, I turn up the radio. The songs

gush into me. I am a country
of such tender lust. A place where birds

deliriously beat their wings, where golden
fish tremble in a lake of tongues.

So I'm Sorry but No, Emily Blunt, I Cannot Make Love to You

Even here, in this dream, in the mouth of this whale built from pink pillows, drifting through a sea of turquoise yarn. Even though you are stretched out in that lingerie of cake icing, I'm sorry, I cannot do it.

Oh, Emily. I can see the hot air balloon rising in your throat. I know you don't just throw yourself at men this way. I feel honored. Really, what an incredible compliment, but I'm sorry. You're going to have to get back on that gigantic lion-headed butterfly and leave through the cupcake orchard you came from.

Oh Emily, no! You mustn't think that, you mustn't! You're perfect! You're dream-perfect, even!

Oh Emily, I bet your lips taste of *dulce de leche*, which is Ice Cream for *the sweetness of milk*, Emily, you are the sweetness of milk and your voice sounds like ladybug rain and your hair sounds like a cup of tea being poured and your skin sounds like a librarian in slow motion and your breasts sound like cathedrals in the snow but I cannot dream myself out of this body.

Even here, my belly slapping into your thighs will sound non-consensual. My shadow will sit on the bookshelf, disgusted, horrified at my bad impression of someone who deserves this, wondering what I'm trying to prove about the nature of beauty; which is your business, Emily, and none of mine.

Rena

Do you see the lady in the moon?
She's screaming. Spraying her lungs across
the Santa Monica night: do you see her
screaming, all silver agony?

I thought I was in love with you,
so yes, yes, I saw everything.

Your bone weapon elbows.
Clarinet wrists. The trenches
where you tried
to cut out the strawberries.

The way you listened to my poems,
it made me long to speak them
inside you.

Together, we watched the dawn
open the sky
with her golden crowbars.

I wished to hold her body in my mouth.
I wished to sing that new light into you,
but you
were already gone.

Oh vapor bandit, frail taker of poems,
the alarms in your wings,
just let them die.

I was screaming *I love you*
so loud I woke up
the part of me that knew I didn't.

That moon thing, look how small it is.
A bead of wax I can scrape away
with a fingernail. A button
that could get lost in the wash.

The night comes again.
The night always comes again.
The night will be the last thing that comes again.

I remember your hands, those shivering
ambulances.

I remember your lips, sleek
as fresh machine guns.

How strange to mourn
the scrapes on your knees
where you hit the ground
to dodge a bullet.

SONS

1.
Your father had no more sons. Your father has one brother. Your father's brother never had children. Your father's father only had sisters. Your grandfather's father was an only child. Your bloodline is a life raft with a gash in the bottom.

Find land.

2.
That night, you crept downstairs,
drank your father's scotch
until your hands stopped shaking,
stumbled outside,
knelt in the dry grass,
fumbled your pants off,
scooped small holes in the soil,
unloaded your seed into them,
prayed and prayed for rain.

3.
At twenty-seven you begin to write a poem called

**SOME DAYS YOU KNOW THAT YOU AND YOUR SON
WILL LOOK AT PICTURES OF ANIMALS AND HE WILL
KNOW MORE OF THEM THAN YOU**

You give up halfway through and write one instead
about a cassowary who falls in love with a linsang.

4.
You are lying next to the girl
who sold you the comic books, tracing her

new initials onto the hushed
smooth of her back. Her freckles

taste like strawberry, she knows
all of the quotes, makes you

laugh like a teakettle
erupting with humming-

birds. Her hair, as red as the red sun
rising in your belly. She has

your daughter's eyes.

So What, Lonely?

"Everybody is making love / or else expecting rain"
-Bob Dylan, "Desolation Row"

No longer will I allow three in the morning to do this:
thread its voice through me like AM radio:
"Visions of Johanna" over and over.
                    So what, lonely?
So what, sad twang guitars? I will not put these coins
in your cups tonight. There is a woman waiting
for me somewhere –
                    her eyes, the color of this,
hair, the color of that. Yes, I am expecting
rain – when it gets here, I will climb it. The clouds
will carry me in their mouths.
                    Because I say she is
gardening, I will wash the soil from her
wrists. She will cup me in her hands, drink me
until I am full.

Poem I Wish I Said to You in High School that One Time When We Were Backstage and You Showed Me that Your Thong Was Zebra Print 'Cause You Saw My Boxers Were Leopard Print and You Said Maybe We Were More Alike Than You Thought

Let me tell you about your shoulders:
they are not shoulders. They are crystal balls – lit
from within. I can see my future. It looks like
your shoulders, smooth as con-men, goose-
bumping beneath my breath.

You played my wife in the second musical I ever did.
It taught me that acting is easy.
All I had to do was look at you.
It also taught me how to sing and dance with a boner.
This is why middle school actors
always bend at the waist to hug or kiss.

Even before you sat on my lap backstage
and told me we had a lot in common,
I knew there was something between us.

If you listen very closely, you can hear a bridge being built
between the way your nose
crinkles up when you laugh
and what will become my lifelong obsession with comedy.

Your laughter
is the sound
of a really hot girl laughing.

At the risk of sounding creepy,
I want to kill your pets
and wear your face as a yarmulke.

KIDDING.

I think about you when I can't sleep,
wishing your head was resting
upon the soft songs
beating against my breastplate.

Shhhhhhhhhh.

I think your boobs are perfect. They make me wish
my hands were seashells.
I think your butt is why my dad yells at me about the water bill.
I think you look like a flushed angel when things get awkward
which I guess means things are always awkward.

O you uncomfortable Jewish masterpiece,
the sexiest thing about you
is that you're no better at this than I am.

Let's accidentally brush pinkies
as we do laps around the mall
until we are accidentally holding hands.
When you tell me that this movie theatre is cold,
know that my mama was a space heater,
my papa was a winter coat.

Neither of us know yet
how the boys will take you for granted
and how the girls
won't take me for anything.

Is it really necessary to find out?

I would rather discover just how slowly I can kiss you,
breathing streaks of fog up and down your spine,
amazed at every curve and ripple

like someone who still thinks it's pronounced
taken for granite
and has no idea what rocks have to do
with something that feels so much like a waterfall.

I will touch the way your slender muscles
point and rush like maps.
I will find my way.
Let me help you find yours:

When you put down this paper, look out the window.
There is a hymn rising like smoke in the south.
Follow it down Valley Circle to Victory,
right turn up a big hill, down a lonesome street
with a trembling streetlight,
second house from the end on your left.

You will find me waiting in a very quiet bedroom.
I will pull you vibrating into my chest.
I will kiss your neck and your earlobes, forever.

All of these poems
will disappear.

WHATEVER THE CASE

"Don't look for a lover, be one"
— James Leo Herlihy

And so, she may be wearing a scarf
in a grove of orange trees

or standing in the doorway
with sunglasses and mouth.

Whatever the case,
I am wearing shoes to dance in

and there are small flowers
fastened to my beard.

And Now, a Word from My Future Wife

Husband,
I know about the hoof-prints crushed into your spine.
Trampled by the low nights, the stillness stampede.
You have thrown yourself beneath them,
again and again.

No more.

I am coming to release you from the mud.
I am coming to bring you into our home.

The flowers you pick for me are shouting
on the nightstand. We will walk through
the orchard, linked, bubbling
like two cans of sweet champagne.
We will catch bullfrogs by the curving stream,
set them loose in the local high school.

I know you think love has been toying with you,
waiting for you to swallow the kitchen knives.

It hasn't.

It wishes only that you would carve a dock
into your sternum. The tide will deliver me.

Husband,
I am coming.

My skin, so soft, you will wish you were mist.
Or spray-on deodorant. Or a loofa.
My shoulders, you will mistake for pianos.
My backbone, a stack of chandeliers.
Your tongue, that ready torch – ignite me.

Your monsters will ask their parents to check under the bed for me.
Your ghosts will tell each other me-stories around the campfire.

I am your worst nightmare's worst nightmare.

Husband,
I am coming.

With my graphic novel attics, infallible Springsteen
lyric retention, Mel Brooks soundtrack of fart routines
and slick Yiddish. We will laugh and make love
and laugh and make love
and you will eat cupcakes out of my palms.

Know that I wear super cute glasses.

Know that I play the banjo.

Know that I make pumpkin pancakes
while dancing in my underwear
every single morning.

Does that sound about right?

Because here you are,
in the same room,
different year,
similar pajama pants,
building me again.

I don't know what else to say to you.

Husband,
go the fuck outside.
Catch up to your life.

I am out there somewhere –
this dark room
is the only place
you will never meet me.

I will not come craving a project.
I will wish to learn you slowly, see
a concert, dance through
the museum, ride your face.

Oh baffled king, oh donkey of sorrow,
you must not confuse me for the eighth grade girls
who were too young to dismiss you carefully.
You must wrench yourself free of that flypaper,
the sticky murder of memory.

When I come, it will not be from the pages
of a comic book.
When I come, I will come
with complications. Acres of bright
hurt, some days, a bucket of scorpions.

I will wish to make your body feel
beautiful with my body. Let me.
I will challenge you to write
a different kind of poem. Let me.
I will forgive you. Let me.

In the meantime, leave your father's house
and live someplace
where you must wash the dishes by hand.
Get a job you hate
and take pride in making
a stranger's life easier.
Learn how to ride a goddamn bicycle.
Memorize the names of flowers,
fish, constellations, people.
Travel.
Kiss someone without thinking
of the future. When you kiss her,
put your whole patience behind it.
When you kiss her,
forget I was ever here.

Slow Dance with Sasquatch

"For who could ever learn to love... a Beast?"
- Narrator, Walt Disney's *Beauty and the Beast*

After we got word of that movie, we all began brushing our fur back
with river water, fastening orchids to our knuckles, wearing tuxedos
stitched of black moss. *They must be coming*, we told each other,
chewing sage and mint to cut the meat from our breath, and *we must be ready
to receive them*. We collected every dead tree
for miles, stripped them with our claws, built a dance floor.
Hung a chandelier of robins' nests and glow worms from the elbow
of an oak. The crickets strummed their legs to the chirping
of the tree frogs; the tree frogs matched the woodpecker's rhythm,
who took his cue from the black bear moaning in her den.
The herons came and taught us to dance, to step lightly, mindful
of delicate things. We had only ever learned trample and snarl,
to be locomotive bearing stockpiles of terror, grinding through farm
girls' nightmares. But what if it was not true? What if there was
gentle in our savage? What if our paws upon a fragile throat
could mean something beautiful? That night, we turned
forest into ballroom. The clouds, alive with light and song.
We waited for them to come. Imagined them in dizzy blue dresses,
skin of sculpted milk, hands light as fog. They would touch our tusks
like piano keys, kiss our dreadlocked shoulders, pull princes
from our bull-goblin bones. We waited

and waited

and waited...

Counting stars
as they fell from the sky
like petals.

Dreaming
we could change back
into something we'd never been.

THANK YOU

It took the support of so many people to make this book, this life, possible. My wildest, howlingest thank yous to:

P. Radin, my pops, the steady miracle. Mama, for seeing all of this noise and translating what it was calling for. Kayla, for too much, too many books and libraries. Always, you are more beautiful. My remarkable family, for being there when I haven't always been. Johnny Auer, there are so many cheeseburgers we have yet to eat together. I miss you. Randi Kearney. Girl. Fierceness and light.

My second family, the True Homies – Scottie D., Mark Saul, Danny Scuderi, Ryan Orenstein, Mike Adams, Lauren I-Can't-Remember-Her-Last-Name, Natalie de Almeida. My untamable gratitude for teaching me to laugh through all this, through everything. Fugitive?

To the teachers who lit me – Sharon Quesnel, Bill Ruehl, Tony Cantrell, Christine Meyer, Terry Fischer, Sue Freitag, Karen Jones, Irene Park, Dave Roberson, Ted Goldenberg. The extraordinary instructors of the Beverly Hills Playhouse – Allen Barton, Art Cohan, Gary Grossman, Milton Katselas, Richard Lawson. None of this without what you've given me.

Alexandra Ella, for the push, the patience. JR Davidson, Brian Elerding, Jorge Garcia, Mike Horton, Roddy Jessup (for the laugh track), Michelle Lawrence, Aaron & Anastasia Leddick, Jimmy Lyons, Audrey Moore, Ashley Platz, Kate Siegel, Samantha Sloyan, Brynn Thayer, Leila Vatan, Jennifer Vo Le, Alex & Fiona Weed, all of MKMW, my glowing engine. They do move in herds!

Kelly Ramel, for the ram jam.

Michelle Nunes, for disproving everything. You are so many armies of butterfly power.

Derrick Brown, for showing me what I wanted to do before I knew I wanted to do it and for responding to a goofy e-mail and for urging me to take off my pants in a bar. Mindy Nettifee, for lunch and then everything, everything, everything after that. Rabbi Shira Erlichman, for maps and courage. Brendan Constantine, Elaina Ellis, Brian S. Ellis, Idris Goodwin, Daniel McGinn, Mike Mcgee, Danielle Mitchell, Jaimes Palacio, Jon Sands, Beau Sia, Amber Tamblyn, G. Murray Thomas, how welcome you have made me feel. Rick Lupert, for watching me suck at this for a long time and thinking of nice things to say. David Gale and Cyrus Sepahbodi, my spirit animals, keeping poetry alive in a quiet place. Candis Kruger, for the panties. Jason Bowe, for the panties. Daniel Lisi, the true King of Westeros, the future, everything is possible. Thank you.

Everyone at Lightbulb Mouth and The Encyclopedia Show Los Angeles and the Dirty Dozen.

Blaine Fontana, for granting me this exceptional cover.

Shea Newkirk, for the rad, fun website.

"The Last Invitation" was written for *The Encyclopedia Show, Los Angeles*

Special thanks to Earl's Donuts, Brent's Deli, and anyone I've forgotten, except Sean Kearney.

ABOUT THE AUTHOR

Jeremy Radin is a poet and actor based out of Los Angeles, where he spends most of his time eating expensive cheeseburgers and thinking about looking for a job. He wrote his first poem because he liked a girl in tenth grade. Don't worry, she never read it... OR ELSE HE'D BE MARRIED. He has performed at several poetry venues in the greater Los Angeles area, co-hosted the original Lightbulb Mouth Radio Hour, co-hosts the rebooted *Lightbulb Mouth, A Literary Adventure*, and is a cast member of *The Encyclopedia Show, Los Angeles*. As an actor, he's spent the last six years studying at the Beverly Hills Playhouse and has appeared on several television shows (*It's Always Sunny in Philadelphia, The Office, Criminal Minds, Unfabulous*). He currently teaches poetry workshops for kids and teens.

JEREMY RADIN'S TOP 10 FAVORITE WB BOOKS

Scandalabra
Former paratrooper Derrick Brown releases a stunning collection of poems written
at sea and in Nashville, TN. About.com's book of the year for poetry.

Rise of the Trust Fall
Award-winning feminist poet Mindy Nettifee
releases her second book of funny, daring, gorgeous, accessible poems.

The Feather Room
Anis Mojgani's second collection of poetry explores storytelling and
poetic form while traveling farther down the path of magic realism.

Racing Hummingbirds
Poet/performer Jeanann Verlee releases an award-winning book
of expertly crafted, startlingly honest, skin-kicking poems.

Write About an Empty Birdcage
Debut collection of poetry from Elaina M. Ellis that flirts with loss,
reveres appetite, and unzips identity.

Yesterday Won't Goodbye
Boston gutter punk Brian Ellis releases his second book of poetry,
filled with unbridled energy and vitality.

1000 Black Umbrellas
Daniel McGinn's first internationally released collection from 'everyone's favorite
unknown author' sings from the guts with the old school power of poetry.

Sunset at the Temple of Olives
Paul Suntup's unforgettable voice merges subversive surrealism
and vivid grief in this debut collection of poetry.

Birthday Girl with Possum
Brendan Constantine's second book of poetry examines the invisible lines
between wonder & disappointment, ecstasy & crime, savagery & innocence.

Ceremony for the Choking Ghost
Slam legend Karen Finneyfrock's second book of poems ventures
into the humor and madness that surrounds familial loss.

NEW WRITE BLOODY BOOKS FOR 2012

Strange Light
The *New York Times* says, "There's something that happens when you read Derrick Brown, a rekindling of faith in the weird, hilarious, shocking, beautiful power of words." This is the final collection from Derrick Brown, one of America's top-selling and touring poets. Everything hilarious and stirring is illuminated. The power of *Strange Light* is waiting.

Who Farted Wrong? Illustrated Weight Loss For the Mind
Syd Butler (of the sweet band, Les Savvy Fav) creates sketchy morsels to whet your appetite for wrong, and it will be delicious. There is no need to read between the lines of this new style of flash thinking speed illustration in this hilarious new book. Why? There are not that many lines.

New Shoes on a Dead Horse
The Romans believed that an artist's inspiration came from a spirit, called a genius, that lived in the walls of the artist's home. This character appears throughout Sierra DeMulder's book, providing charming commentary and biting insight on the young author's creative process and emotional path.

Good Grief
Elegantly-wrought misadventures as a freshly-graduated Michigan transplant, Stevie Edwards stumbles over foal legs through Chicago and kneels down to confront the wreckage of her skinned knees.

After the Witch Hunt
Megan Falley showcases her fresh, lucid poetry with a refreshing lack of jaded undertones. Armed with both humor and a brazen darkness, each poem in this book is another swing of the pick axe in this young woman's tunnel, insistent upon light.

I Love Science!
Humorous and thought provoking, Shanney Jean Maney's book effortlessly combines subjects that have previously been thought too diverse to have anything in common. Science, poetry and Jeff Goldblum form covalent bonds that put the poetic fire underneath our bunsen burners. A Lab Tech of words, Maney turns language into curious, knowledge-hungry poetry. Foreword by Lynda Barry.

Time Bomb Snooze Alarm
Bucky Sinister, a veteran poet of the working class, layers his gritty truths with street punk humor. A menagerie of strange people and stranger moments that linger in the dark hallway of Sinister's life. Foreword by Randy Blythe of "Lamb of God".

News Clips and Ego Trips
A collection of helpful articles from *Next...* magazine, which gave birth to the Southern California and national poetry scene in the mid-'90s. It covers the growth of spoken word, page poetry and slam, with interviews and profiles of many poets and literary giants like Patricia Smith, Henry Rollins and Miranda July. Edited by G. Murray Thomas.

Slow Dance With Sasquatch
Jeremy Radin invites you into his private ballroom for a waltz through the forest at the center of life, where loneliness and longing seamlessly shift into imagination and humor.

The Smell of Good Mud
Queer parenting in conservative Oklahoma, Lauren Zuniga finds humor and beauty in this collection of new poems. This explores the grit and splendor of collective living, and other radical choices. It is a field guide to blisters and curtsies.

WRITE BLOODY ANTHOLOGIES

The Elephant Engine High Dive Revival (2009)
Our largest tour anthology ever! Features unpublished work by
Buddy Wakefield, Derrick Brown, Anis Mojgani and Shira Erlichman!

The Good Things About America (2009)
American poets team up with illustrators to recognize the beauty and wonder in our
nation. Various authors. Edited by Kevin Staniec and Derrick Brown

Junkyard Ghost Revival (2008)
Tour anthology of poets, teaming up for a journey of the US in a small van.
Heart-charging, socially active verse.

The Last American Valentine:
Illustrated Poems To Seduce And Destroy (2008)
Acclaimed authors including Jack Hirschman, Beau Sia, Jeffrey McDaniel,
Michael McClure, Mindy Nettifee and more. 24 authors and 12 illustrators
team up for a collection of non-sappy love poetry. Edited by Derrick Brown

Learn Then Burn (2010)
Exciting classroom-ready anthology for introducing new writers
to the powerful world of poetry. Edited by Tim Stafford and Derrick Brown.

Learn Then Burn Teacher's Manual (2010)
Tim Stafford and Molly Meacham's turn key classroom-safe guide
to accompany *Learn Then Burn*: A modern poetry anthology for the classroom.

Knocking at the Door: Poems for Approaching the Other (2011)
An exciting compilation of diverse authors that explores the concept of the Other
from all angles. Innovative writing from emerging and established poets.

WRITEBLOODY

WWW.WRITEBLOODY.COM

Pull Your Books Up
By Their Bootstraps

Write Bloody Publishing distributes and promotes great books of fiction, poetry and art every year. We are an independent press dedicated to quality literature and book design, with an office in Long Beach, CA.

Our employees are authors and artists so we call ourselves a family. Our design team comes from all over America: modern painters, photographers and rock album designers create book covers we're proud to be judged by.

We publish and promote 8-12 tour-savvy authors per year. We are grass-roots, D.I.Y., bootstrap believers. Pull up a good book and join the family. Support independent authors, artists and presses.

Visit us online:

WRITEBLOODY.COM

NOTES, GROCERY LISTS & DOODLES:

CPSIA information can be obtained at www.ICGtesting.com
Printed in the USA
BVOW072033020613

322194BV00001B/3/P